Y0-EKP-854

TRUE TALES
OF
GHOSTS

TRUE TALES

OF

GHOSTS

S.L. Vadimsky   C.L. Vadimsky

Contents

Millions of spiritual creatures walk
the earth,

Unseen, both when we wake and when
we sleep.

—John Milton, *Paradise Lost*

Preface

These collected stories are told in the words of witnesses. We stated "just the facts", without speculation as to the origin or cause of the hauntings. We leave that to your imagination.

Of course, even though the experiences and memories of eyewitnesses are theirs, once told and retold and handed down around the fire or the water cooler, they become shared histories, belonging too to those who listened with wonder.

As Nathaniel Hawthorne cautions: "Nobody has any conscience about adding to the improbabilities of a marvelous tale."

Acknowledgements

We thank our family, friends, colleagues and neighbors for sharing their experiences with us for this book, and for supporting our endeavors always, especially Brian, Elizabeth, Greg, Gordon, Jim, John, Kristina, Richard, Stephanie, and Sue.

We also acknowledge with respect the beings who lived before and visit from another time or place.

TRUE TALES

OF

GHOSTS

"...and if you don't mind a ghost in the house, it's all right. Only you must remember I warned you."

—Oscar Wilde,
            The Canterville Ghost

ELMER

I t was the summer after my first year in college. My newly divorced mother moved into a second-floor apartment in a weathered gray house on a tree-lined street in an old neighborhood in Catasauqua, Pennsylvania. The landlords, husband and wife, told my mother about Elmer who once lived in the house with his wife, his high-school sweetheart. As the story goes, Elmer watched football on television every Monday night. Late in life, when his beloved wife could no longer care for him, Elmer was moved into a nursing home. His body, and soon his mind, quickly deteriorated and so he didn't understand when the nurse told him that his wife had died. It wasn't long before he, too, passed on.

A few sets of renters had lived there before my mother, but they all moved out at the end of the term without renewing their rental agreement. But the landlord assured my mom, "Elmer doesn't ever cause any trouble. The last renter told us Elmer returns every Monday night looking for his wife. But no trouble."

It wasn't until after my mom signed the lease that the landlord added that Elmer also made noises, walked down the hallway, turned water on and off, and banged pots and pans in the kitchen. Oh, and that their particular block was built near an old burial site. The Lenni Lenape.

My mom wondered if the spirits were upset, possibly vengeful, or at least giving Elmer some assistance in navigating the spirit world.

My mom didn't seem to have any trepidation about living in a haunted house. Perhaps she didn't want to instill fear in me, as we'd thrown around the idea of my moving in with her for the summer. It sounded like a great idea to me, but first I had to see about this "Elmer the football fan", and what it felt like to sleep there overnight. I had always felt things: energies, spirits. Sometimes they were my ancestors and sometimes complete strangers whose intentions I couldn't discern.

So I packed a bag of some clothes and my guitar and went to mom's for a week-long trial run. The place was still full of unpacked boxes on the kitchen counter and along the bedroom walls. That first night was fine, as was the second. In fact, the whole week was fine. Sure, we heard a few noises, just house noises, and maybe looked at each other blankly a few times when a strong breeze blew through the window screen. But we just laughed it away by having a fake conversation with Elmer. "Hi, Elmer. We're moving in, we don't mean to bother you. Your wife isn't here, by the way. But you can watch TV." All was well.

Now for some reason, my mother went away the following weekend when I had planned to move in my bed and dresser and a few boxes of my important things. Fine. In fact, I was thrilled to have the place to myself. I'd have a friend over whose older brother would buy us beer. We'd eat pizza, play loud music, and feel like adults.

It just so happened that the middle room, my mom's room, where I'd sleep until I set up my bed the following day, was much darker than my room. Mine was in the front of the house that looked down on the street. Bright

6

sunshine poured through the tall front pane windows. Dingy floral wallpaper peeled off the plaster walls and the scuffed hardwood floors creaked. My room. It felt good. Mostly. Until I opened what I thought was the closet door. I lifted the bolt, slid it to the left, slowly pulled the door open and peered in. Nope. Steps and cobwebs. Attic. I quickly shut the door and slid the bolt back and never opened it again.

My mom's room had an old glass chandelier that hung from the center of the ceiling. The two windows in the room opened to the northeast side just 15 feet from the neighbor's house. Tall trees in the yard and the neighbor's roof line blocked the sun most of the day. Of all the rooms in the house, this room definitely felt the heaviest. Now I was well aware that my mind was set up to feel ghostly things, but the air really seemed thick, damp and cold. No doubt it used to be Elmer's and his wife's bedroom.

But it was fine. Nothing had happened the week before.

After spending the day unpacking, exploring the backyard, raiding the fridge, and talking to friends on the phone, I changed into my night clothes, poured a glass of water and went to bed. I set the half-empty glass on the nightstand next to the lamp and crawled under my mom's familiar sheets and lay there staring at the ceiling.

Soon, my eyes grew heavy and I drifted off to sleep. After some unrecorded amount of time, my eyes burst open and I held my breath. What the--? I heard rattling right next to me. My thoughts jumped back and forth and up and down, trying to make sense of what was happening. The rattling continued, getting louder and more forceful. I knew this sound. Yes, that's it! The sound of my drinking glass clanging against the glass shade of the antique lamp. I heard it earlier when I set my water glass down. Slowly I turned my head and looked toward the lamp. In a split second I saw what I saw, without a doubt—the nightstand was shaking! I threw the covers over my head, wide-eyed in the dark, frozen. The shaking and rattling stopped after about twenty seconds. All was still. Quiet. Except my pounding heart.

Looking back now, I realize I did something I had done so many times before and that I would do again and again throughout my life when faced with intense fear. I shut down. I don't know how I did it, but I immediately put myself to sleep as if I had simply flicked a switch. It was a deep sleep. Safe. Protected. I didn't wake up until morning. The sun shone. A gentle summer breeze blew through the screen. Everything was fine.

Maybe Elmer realized we weren't all that bad, as embodied renters go, and he found no need or pleasure in scaring us anymore. Maybe he even felt a little guilty for shaking that table, an overreaction perhaps, defensiveness. It's hard to know what ghosts feel and why they do what they do. Whatever his reasons he mellowed down by midsummer and my mom and I settled into this living arrangement. We went about our daily lives, mom going to work and navigating her new unmarried life, and me, doing everything possible to have fun before I had to go back to college in September. We supposed Elmer, too, went about his days being ghostly.

The three of us seemed to have found a certain harmony. We acknowledged him, treated him with a certain respect, I guess. Like late at night when he banged pots and pans in the kitchen. "Elmer? Hello? We can hear you. Don't forget to turn the stove off." He never used the stove, but our playing, our pretending, seemed to relieve our fears.

I have no idea what kind of person Elmer was when he had a body, (serious? funny? simple-minded, quick-witted?), but it seemed that he acknowledged us by playing with us, too. Like when we'd be in the kitchen and we'd hear running water from the bathroom which was on the other side of the kitchen wall. One of us would go into the bathroom to investigate, only to hear the water now coming from the kitchen.

The first time this happened was unbelievable. Our brains could not accept the data. We both kept going back and forth between the kitchen and the bathroom like little children being deceived by parental "magic" tricks, our mouths wide open, eyes bulging. After two or three more times of playing this game, like the banging pots, we got used to running water.

One afternoon when I'd borrowed her car, my mother asked me to pick her up at work. A storm was headed our way, so she reminded me to close all the windows before I left, every single one, even the sticky ones in the hallway.

When we returned 45 minutes later, the rain hadn't started but the wind blew strong. I was first to climb the half-dozen steps and reach the front door. I put the key in the lock, turned it, pushed open the door and walked onto the landing at the foot of the stairs leading up to our apartment.

My mom was right behind me as I started to climb the staircase. "I thought I asked you to close the windows," mom scolded.

"I did!"

Almost simultaneously, we both blurted, "Elmer!"

I added, "Not funny, Elmer."

That same night after dinner, we decided to play cards, as we often did. We went through our usual games: crazy eights, rummy, gin rummy, go fish. Elmer would turn on the water in the bathroom. We'd laugh and ask him to turn it off. He did. For some reason that evening I decided to record our fun and games on my new mini-cassette recorder. It was a habit of mine. Like taking photographs, I liked capturing moments with my friends and family on tape, to listen in the future and remember all the fun we'd had.

But this time, after my mom and I had our fill of cards, I wanted to rewind the recorder and listen back right then and there, knowing there were some pretty funny moments. So back we went to relive the fun. We listened and laughed at all the same places we'd laughed the first time.

Then, after a few minutes of this, we heard something that we couldn't believe was real. But there it was. On tape. During one of our games of go fish, I had asked my mom if she had a queen of hearts. And in the space between my asking and her answering, a low male voice said, "Queen of hearts, queen of hearts." Our mouths dropped open.

We kept rewinding the tape and playing it again and again.

CAPTURED

ON FILM

I live and work in a very old town, established by Dutch and English colonists before the American Revolutionary War which formed the United States. It lay halfway on the very old road between New York and Philadelphia. Over time, houses continued to be built in the town which became the county seat, a center of business, a railroad crossroads. There are

beautiful but expensive to maintain examples
of architecture from the 1800s and from the
1920s, as well as a few simpler structures
dating back to the War, where General
Washington maintained quarters. The tree on
Hangman's Hill was finally removed at some
point, and a few townhouses went up nearby,
just skirting the unfortunate clearing on the
Hill.

I know about houses because I am a real
estate appraiser. We have to measure, inspect
and photograph houses, inside and out, and
estimate the home's value, for bank loans and
other purposes. Sometimes there are peculiar
intimate details in a home, which the
homeowner is bold enough to leave out in the
open, soiled clothing, guns, most commonly
friendly or hostile watch dogs. None of these
is relevant to the home's value, and so I
maintain no record of these; in fact, I am
obliged to avoid recording the people who live
in the house and in the neighborhood.

One pleasantly clear, dry day, I was appraising a fine old Federal style house on High Street. I duly inspected and photographed the interior. Each room, including the kitchen, was clean and dry and orderly. Nothing was cooking, the heat was not running, there were no shadows, no dappling sun. Of course the floors creaked throughout the house, echoing my steps, its being a very old house. I completed my work in the final room, the kitchen, left the house and went on my way.

Those were the days of film processing, so I created my sketch, performed calculations, and wrote the report, then picked up the developed photographs.

There was something wrong about the kitchen photograph. A dense fog or cloud of mist or condensation hung in the kitchen between the countertops and table. It hovered about six feet high and a couple feet wide. There was nothing wrong with any of the other photos on the roll, but in each photo of the kitchen, there the gray cloud appeared. I wracked my brain for an explanation—moisture, a flaw in my camera, a smudge? Weather conditions, a cold camera lens? I had used the same equipment in numerous houses, in every kind of condition, and this was the only house which showed this effect. No answer seemed satisfactory. I had to put in my report a note to disregard the artifact in the photograph *which was not observed* during the real time inspection of the premises, and went on with my other professional work, dismissing the matter from my memory.

Appraisers often find themselves returning to a house in the future for other appraisals. It tends to be a small circle of appraisers familiar with an area and whose work is accepted by bank clients, to whom the banks turn first. As it happens, some time later I had an order to return to appraise the same High Street Federal house.

Same fine weather. Same steps through the house and same inspection. This appraisal was for new owners, and there had been renovation and updating of the kitchen, but otherwise the same empty, orderly room, no appliances in use. I carefully assessed the lighting and my camera. I looked around outside for any source of reflection. I completed my work, and completed the report at my office.

I picked up the photos and reviewed them immediately.

Same cloud of mist was there, in the kitchen. In each angle of the picture, it appeared in a different place in the room and in the photograph. I again had to note in the appraisal report regarding this phenomenon:

Note: The apparent undefined grayish fog appearing in the kitchen photograph was not observed by this appraiser during the onsite inspection. It is presumed to be an artifact caused by the camera or film

19

development. A conclusive determination of the cause is beyond the scope of work for this assignment.

The next time I received an order to perform an appraisal of this house, (when the house had changed hands a third time in as many years), I declined the job.

NANCY

HOLDS MY HAND

A s a "sensitive" or "psychic", I can interact with the spirit world on a very basic level. I used to dabble in astral projection and did some work as a medium, but after an encounter with a powerful negative entity, I no longer seek out paranormal experiences, especially with spirits with whom I'm not familiar. However, that doesn't mean that they don't find me.

I have the pleasure of working at one of the most beautiful historical sites in New Jersey. On a typical day, I get to educate groups of school children about local history and field interesting and thoughtful questions about how people lived in our nation's past.

What the children don't know is that once they're seated on their big yellow buses and we've waved them goodbye, the historical site, with its four-story, 19th century grist mill, its tenant house and quarry, its antique exhibits winding over ten acres of land, is haunted by the spirits of people long past.

The proprietors of the mill offer adult "ghost tours" in the evenings, starting at dusk and ending once the sky is black and the lights of the nearby town are warm and welcoming. These tours are given by staff members and a local group of ghost hunters who know the tales of the old buildings and are all too happy to leave tourists with a nervous shiver.

I had never been on one of the ghost tours, even after working there during daytime hours for several years, so one afternoon I asked my brother if he would come with me. I dearly love my historic workplace, and always relish the opportunity to share it with friends and family. My brother, a skeptic at best, agreed, and we set out for the tour.

The mill is of course on a river, which made the power used to turn its great stone wheel, first for the production of wool and then to grind feed, flour and stone from the quarry. We stood with the group in the cold, dark first floor of the mill building, where the millstones and machinery were kept during the building's years of operation. Our host treated us to some facts about the mill's history and about the many people who had passed through these walls over the centuries. We learned that a structure's proximity to water is said to bear spiritual significance, according to some traditions. We walked through the first floor and headed upstairs, a path I typically traveled in my school tours.

Everything is always different at night, though. Even the familiar. I remember how dark everything in the space felt, like there were blackout curtains draped around the exhibits I knew so well. I knew they were there but could see only blackness, not a glint of reflected light.

The first floor of the mill is actually below ground, so not much light gets in through the small, high windows, even in broad daylight. With the sun rapidly setting, you can imagine just how dark it was. Still, I wasn't afraid; this wasn't my first time visiting the dark corners of the mill, after all, since I'd worked here in the winter and had seen the buildings after dark. And I was familiar with how the mill's atmosphere felt.

If you accept the truth of paranormal phenomena, you'll no doubt be familiar with the description of haunted places. For the sensitive, the difference between a haunted place and an ordinary place doesn't necessarily feel foreboding, unless there's a negative spirit lurking. Some say the air will feel cold or heavy. I live in a house that isn't haunted. At home the air feels clean, uninterrupted.

But the mill and its buildings just felt "different". In the mill, the air feels like you're walking through a spider web or a silk curtain. The change isn't much, but it's enough that you notice it.

My brother and I followed the tour group upstairs to the second floor of the mill. I'm very familiar with this area and its exhibits, since most tour groups spend the most time in this area. Before the mill had stairs, there were trap doors through which a ladder could be used for people to climb up and down, and a pulley system for transporting material between floors. I delight in telling children about the trap door near the miller's office replica by the back stairs; there's always either a frightened response, where the kids clamor to get off the trap door, or an excited response, where the brave try to jump on it to make it open. (It won't; trap doors in places like this actually opened up, not down. This isn't an old cartoon, after all.)

It was during this part of the tour that I became acquainted with a new spirit.

The tour guide began his story about visitors who had seen the ghost of a little girl. Long ago, she had come to the mill with her father who worked there. The girl fell down through the opened trap door, tragically dying from her fall to the first floor. The gift shop now occupies the place of her fatal injury.

As the guide was relating the tale, I suddenly felt a presence beside me. I've worked with children for years, and I cared for a young cousin, five years old at the time, so I know what it feels like when a child stands right next to you in order to get your attention. I looked down and saw golden curls and a light-colored dress.

There were no children on this tour, and certainly not any half shrouded from my view, as the ghosts I see often are. I looked away from her, since she seemed shy, and offered her my open hand, allowing her the chance to interact.

She did. I felt a tiny hand clasp mine, tiny fingers nestling in between my palm and thumb. It was so brief that I could have convinced myself that I was dreaming. I was no longer paying attention to the tour guide; this experience was much more important. The name "Nancy" came into my mind, and I sensed that this was the name she wanted to be called.

Then she was gone. By this time, the tour group was moving on, but I felt changed by this experience. The moon and starlight rippled on the water and I shivered, but that was probably just the blast of cool autumn air as we exited the dense dark mill.

After that night, I started seeing Nancy at the mill more often. She never spoke, but I would see her out of the corner of my eye, peeking out from behind doors on the second floor, or, rarely, sneaking in between my kids in tour groups. I made it a point to say hello to her. After all, she must have felt very lonely, as the only ghost child on the property, as far as I know.

It's strange, but I miss her now. The mill closed to visitors for a time due to a public health emergency, and I haven't been back to the site for a long while. I often wonder about how the ghosts feel, having the old buildings to themselves, and whether or not they miss the activity of the living.

Does Nancy miss me, just like I miss her?

TURNING

THE PAGES

After the Second World War, in the eastern part of Europe, everything had been destroyed. Then the Russians came and took all the provisions. There was nothing to plant, and there was much hunger.

In the remote village in the mountains where my mother grew up, the road had not even been paved yet. No buses came to her town. It was uncommon for people to come all the way to visit this village to sell supplies.

But on occasion during the season, a visitor would come to a town not so far away to sell cherries.

One such day, when my mother was a girl, she set off with a friend on a long walk to the town to buy some cherries.

Now at the time, the people would dry the grass in hay stacks built around a stick. The hay would be used to feed the livestock. My mom and her friend walked down the unpaved road past the haystacks.

She shaded her eyes and looked at one of the stacks. On one of the stacks, she saw a very old lady. She did not know the lady, but the woman looked far too old and frail to be out in the field. And the oddest thing about her, which made my mother stare, was that she was just sitting there reading a book.

Now this was very odd because very few people could read at that time in that place, and especially, old women had never learned to read, being from another time, and being women, busy with family and farm.

My mother marveled at this sight but kept it to herself, thinking with longing of the cherries at the end of their travels.

Even though her village was poor then, and hungry, it was a very beautiful village. You walk through turns in the road up a hill and then down, and when you walk over the hill and down, you spy a lovely town. The best view of all isn't in the village where they lived and worked, no, the best view was from the church cemetery on the hill. From there, their dead could look down over the sparklingly beautiful valley, for eternity.

As she and her friend kept walking to town, my mother suddenly felt dizzy and nauseated and she had to stop, as she felt very sick all over. Suddenly a great wind rose and blew over them. As she looked out over the road, she saw a very beautiful lady in a beautiful dress of many all-over colors. This lady came twirling, spinning, out of the field next to them, and spun across their road, and continued spinning up and down over the hills, until she crossed the top of a hill out of sight. As soon as the lady in the colorful, twirling dress was gone from sight, my mother felt her sickness pass.

Well this she knew for sure, that she had seen a fairy. In our country, and indeed in many lands, everyone well knew that fairies do not walk anywhere. Fairies are over-fond of dancing, and fairies travel by twirling, spinning. As a result they can generate wind. Maybe they could even make you dizzy to see them.

When the girls went home she told her parents about her adventures. Her parents

were shocked by her vision of the old woman
reading a book. At that very moment when my
mother saw the old lady with the book at the
haystack, was when an old, bedridden lady in
the village had died. The old woman had
never learned to read, but it seemed that in
death, her spirit must have acquired some
kind of knowledge from some book.

As for the fairy, was she connected in
some way with the old woman's spirit? Who
could say? Perhaps the old woman's book was
a special gift from the fairy, to whom she had
once done a kindness. Or was the old woman's
death caused by her old heart's surprise at
some trick in a fairy visitation?

Maybe there was no connection at all
between the two, except for my mother's
witness. It may be that her path just happened
to cross that of these beings going earnestly or
frivolously about their separate business,
among many others. For whatever reason, the
veil between my mother's daily existence and
the movements of the beings in the other

world, had slipped or become thin enough to see through.

My mother marvels still at these visions of hers, because since growing up, she has been only a very practical woman, busy with sensible things.

THE HAUNTED

HOTEL

AND MY HEART

P erhaps you have heard of Salem.

My family visits Salem, Massachusetts, every now and then. My mother's an English major. She loves the New England coastal towns and New England history. In Salem a lovely tall ship is moored, the Friendship. The

Friendship is a recreated Salem East Indiaman built in Salem in 1797. The original was captured by the British on her way back from Russia and no one knows what became of her.

Ships, like hurricanes, were once called feminine pronouns, but we know better now.

The Salem Maritime National Historic Site was the first national historic site ever made, on March 17, 1938. Before that, it was located in a house on the site of the Hawthorne Hotel, in a house which had since burned down.

You can also see Nathaniel Hawthorne's House of the Seven Gables here; well, the house that inspired the novel. It is black outside, the way the cedar houses at the shore are black from age and weather.

When we were there, the waterfront was sunny and cold and we saw a rainbow over the Friendship. Then we walked a cobblestone road and went back to our hotel for the night, the Hawthorne Hotel. It was our first night.

You know about the witch trials. Those happened mostly outside the town, in what was then Salem Village, (now called Danvers, Mass.). You know they weren't really witches, right. Some girls behaved very strangely like they were possessed or bewitched, their conduct was contagious and as a group, one after another, they accused older women they knew, and a few good men, too. The adults were wrongly accused of witchcraft and tried and killed, or killed *by* trial. There is a very moving graveyard park memorializing every one of the innocent accused dead.

These days, oddly, even though the original witches weren't really witches, many modern witches flock to Salem and tourists come to celebrate witchcraft. Maybe because even though the accused witches weren't really real witches, there is really no one satisfactory explanation for how the afflicted girls behaved. Accidental poisoning, hysteria, avoiding punishments by Puritanical parents...

Anyway, this was my first night in Salem. My sister and I hadn't even been to the witch trial show yet, or the witch museum. I was a kid. My summer travel baseball season had ended. It had been a good season, though hot and dusty. Mom was treating us, and herself, to a short vacation and Salem was just a stop on the way to see *Moby Dick* and *Perfect Storm* history in Gloucester. We were always up for a good vacation with lots of eating out for me and lots of gift shop doodads which were my sister's interest. She was all about the magic wands and crystals and stuff in this town.

Other than Elizabeth's gift shop toy dabbling, my family does not believe in paranormal things. I am now a scientist.

I was born with a hole in my heart. My mom says I screamed all the time either because of the hole, or because, as I remember it, I was hungry. She held my heart to hers and I grew out of it. I am a healthy man now. And I was a normal boy when I was in Salem then.

The Hawthorne Hotel is near a hundred years old, from back in the 1920's. Before that it was a house, and that house burned down multiple times.

Supposedly now there is a giant Halloween party there every year and the rooms cost a fortune, but rooms at the Hawthorne Hotel in midsummer were dirt cheap, as the hotel was empty. The huge lobby had stuffed upholstered furniture and potted palms and we could sit anywhere. It was more like a grand house, really. We had our meals, (the highlight for me), right there in the restaurant in a corner of the downstairs lobby.

We went upstairs to our rooms on the sixth floor early. No one else was in the hallway, but there was a small man glaring at us as he was opening a strange kind of closet at the end of the hall. Usually when we stayed in nice hotels the housekeeping staff and managers smiled cheerily and said, "good day" if you caught them in the hallway, even if they were caught in the middle of something like gossip or an argument about hours or a smoke. But this man turned his head to us and glared, and he wouldn't look away, even as he was shoving or yanking something deep in the closet. It was a strange closet, like maybe it had been a dumbwaiter once. He was small and thick-armed, with black hairy eyebrows and a mop of black hair low on his forehead, and he grunted and glared. My mom quickly looked away and rushed us into our rooms, next to his closet.

"Well, that's New England. People can be stingy with words. They don't feel obliged to welcome you. It doesn't mean they are actually hostile." Mother observed the closer to Boston one was, the more Irish or Anglo-Saxon many people appear, and then as one wends north]]]in the direction of Canada, more people are small, dark and French, perhaps.

We immediately took our dog out, and the man was gone. There was no one else anywhere on the floor.

The long drive we'd had today, and the long walk to the rainbow and back, helped me fall asleep fast in the adjoining room to my mom's and sister's.

Then I awoke in the dark. It must have been the middle of the night. The bright hallway light shone under the crack in the door. I heard a racket in the hallway, like people walking sloppily down the hall, but there were no voices, or shadows under the door as they passed.

My mom snored. For this reason, my sister slept with her head phones on, playing her music all night. I knew she couldn't hear anything. I closed my eyes tightly but could not get back to sleep.

I suddenly became aware of a woman standing over me. She pressed her two hands onto my chest over my heart and leaned into it. I was afraid to open my eyes, but I knew it was a woman, and I felt her hands pressing down, pressing my chest in. In the next room our dog was growling, and I heard my mom trying to soothe the dog with a treat. Our dog went wild with growling and barking and the woman's hands were suddenly gone. I felt lighter.

Mom and the dog went back to silence. I opened my eyes. I didn't see anything but I was afraid to turn the light on to look for sure, and I couldn't fall asleep again.

The next day at breakfast, after checkout, I told my mom. She opened her eyes wide.

"I hadn't wanted to scare you, and wasn't going to say anything until we were leaving. But wouldn't you know it, in an empty hotel, they put us in that room! I had a funny feeling when we went up there and I researched it online. Supposedly the floor is haunted—wouldn't you know! They gave us the most haunted room! I wouldn't open my eyes all night, even when that racket of footsteps rolled down the hallway. I was beside myself when Nanny was growling!"

My sister said, "That's pretty weird because in my head phones last night, the music suddenly disappeared and all I could hear through them was a woman screaming! I thought it must be coming from the hallway and that someone must be terribly hurt. But when I sat up and took off my headset, there was just silence." We all looked at each other with eyebrows raised.

Then mom handled the bill and we packed the car. I looked back at the empty lot as we drove away. It really was a beautiful house and a beautiful town, in the sunshine.

I've done the research now too. Perhaps I had experienced the Night Hag. Many cultures have witnessed the waking to a woman sitting on or pressing on one's chest. The feeling is the height and weight of a woman.

Was she drawn to me because of some scar over the hole in my heart? Was she a tender guardian, or did she hunger for my weakness?

All I can find about the ghosts experienced by other hotel residents is reference to a woman on the sixth floor...

THE THREE

WOMEN

I am an aging and experienced lawyer, historian and artist. I am an atheist. I believe in the forces of history and economics. My wife and our son are also atheists. I can argue all day explaining to Christians how they are deluded. I can argue why moral atheists exhibit superior morality in their thoughts and actions, without religious belief, and why our world would be better if religion were extinguished. I was not raised as a Catholic, nor was my wife. Our families of origin were of other faiths. We did not espouse the recognition of Catholic "saints".

I suffer from chronic physical illness, one or more autoimmune disorders. To govern my condition to keep me working and active full-time, I abstain from many foods and all recreational or therapeutic substance use such as drugs or alcohol.

I share this story with very few people because I am afraid people will misunderstand me. I don't even understand what happened to me. But I have not found religion as a result of this experience, even if the experience is evidence of existence beyond our mortal understanding.

During one of my most uncomfortable attacks of illness, I experienced something. The strangest aspect of this experience is that I did not experience it as a dream while asleep, or as a vision or appearance. I was awake, conscious, thinking and feeling my ordinary surroundings, and I experienced the fact of three women becoming present with me. They transported me through space, through outer space, past stars and planets.

I know this is not possible. But it happened, and I witnessed this. They showed me the deepest universe as a backdrop to their presence. The women said they were Saint Elizabeth, Saint Mary and Another. They told me not to fear my life or my death. They told me there was more than all this.

When they returned me to my ordinary surroundings and left me, I knew I had experienced some profound sight beyond the curtain of our daily routine understanding of ourselves.

I do not know what to make of this. I have absolutely no doubt that this was no illusion, hallucination, or creation of my own. I know this was a visitation from elsewhere, and I have faith in this experience. It has not changed my habits of worship, but I am a different man now. I work hard as always serving others, I suffer pain and disabilities sometimes, but I have no fear.

MRS. MICKS

To this day, my wife finds me yelling at Mrs. Micks in my sleep.

Back when I was a teenager in the 70's, my mother and stepfather were looking to buy a house. Before they bought the house, my mother had taken us kids to look it over. No one lived there, it was the estate of a dead woman with no living family.

After my mom completed the purchase of the house, she reminded us of the visit, and asked if we had removed anything from boxes left in the attic of the house? We had not. My mom just looked puzzled.

When we arrived at the house to move in, my sister and I eagerly went in first. We stopped in the entryway and heard really ominous noises, banging, someone moaning. Something sounded like a howling, "Whooooooooooooo..." Then it stopped.

"What was that?"

We looked at each other and shrugged it off. After all, we didn't know the neighborhood. Maybe there was, I don't know, some kind of work being done, a siren or whistle like that, or something?

The Attic

As we moved in, we were cleaning the whole house. My mother and I finished in the attic and had everything all clean and tidy. Our extra things were neatly stored. We went downstairs in satisfaction. But I suddenly remembered, I'd forgotten to turn off the attic light, so I went up to check.

Strangely, all of our neatly folded blankets had been unfolded and laid out in the middle of the floor. I put them away again, shaking my head in confusion, and turned out the light when I left.

We soon found out about the occupant of our house from a neighbor. Mrs. Micks had lived in the house, which her husband had built for her on an empty lot. After he died, she lived in the house all alone with her many generations of cats.

She had been found, long dead, in the attic of the house, where she had been food for her desperate cats, neglected since her death.

Once we were moved in and living there, we often heard noises in the attic. A few weeks after we moved in, we investigated one such crash. A book shelf had been knocked over.

Even stranger, a kind of "pirate chest" which had been up there, was standing against the wall as usual, but it was open. The clothing and other contents stored in the chest had all been removed and were dumped out in the middle of the floor!

My mother used to dry peppers in the attic on a string across the room. Once, we found five peppers laid out in a perfect circle on the floor. The holes in the pepper used to string them up had not been ripped. It was as if someone had untied the string, slipped the peppers off, and hung the line back where it was.

We had roofers to the house to repair the roof. They had a ladder propped in a hole in the roof, feet on the attic floor. One of them went to step onto it to go down, and discovered the ladder had been removed and was lying on the floor. That was a risky trick, Mrs. Micks, someone might have been hurt!

When the roofers left, they couldn't find one of their brand-new crowbars, and asked us if it turned up, to let them know. We found it three months later hidden in the bottom drawer of an old dresser in the attic!

Lost and Found

We started to find that whenever something went missing, a TV remote control, tools put down for a moment, keys, the kind of misplaced stuff you find in your couch cushions when you go looking—we could find it in the attic, stuffed into the crawlspace between the walls and rafters.

We even found a cleaver up there, not ours. Whatever had she been chopping up in the attic?

And sometimes, just when you would go out and buy a replacement for something you couldn't find anywhere, the missing item would be restored to its place after all.

We took to shaking our fists and yelling, "that Mrs. Micks!" But we didn't feel threatened, it was just sort of a feature of our house.

Once my mom was wrapping a present with gift wrap and when she went in the other room, the whole thing disappeared. She was irritated and swore at Mrs. Micks. Upon her words, there followed a loud boom! And a decorative plate, displayed on the moulding shelf around the room, rattled, shook, and fell.

Mrs. Micks Messes with Us

Like Mrs. Micks, my mom fostered kittens. Even guests would notice the way our kittens' eyes would jointly track something rising, rising, rising, until the kittens fell over backward. They would all play with something invisible to us, but clearly they all recognized the one point in space in which this playmate existed.

I was often at home alone, me and the animals, after school while everyone else worked, and Mrs. Micks would mess with me. I would be doing my homework in my bedroom and the cat would look up at the ceiling. Sure enough, there would be a crash in the attic.

Once I was listening to records in my room, and the needle arm suddenly scratched across the surface of the record and hit the center spindle, as if someone had flicked it. I restored it and after a short while the same thing happened again. I felt a chill behind me and the hairs on my neck stood on end.

I ran out of the house and waited on the porch for the rest of the family!

Often, I had chores assigned to me to do after school. One day it was my turn to vacuum. A canister vacuum cleaner was stored on the landing where the stairs turned. When I went halfway up to that landing and tried to grab the handle hose to bring it downstairs, it was stuck and I couldn't pull it. Something or someone was pulling the other end away from me. I saw a shadow moving on the wall and I turned and ran outside, locked the door and sat on the porch.

When my mom got home, she laughed, "Mrs. Micks again?"

The dogs didn't like that landing either, and we figured that Mrs. Micks must not like dogs. Our dogs slept on the landing to be near as possible to us whether we were upstairs or down, but they flat out refused to go one step further upstairs, the whole time we lived in the house.

Contact

One night the adults were out, and my gang of friends came over to hang with me and keep me company.

We were not a superstitious bunch, which is why we had no fear of the Ouija board among our other games, as so many people do. My friends didn't even believe anything we had told them about Mrs. Micks; they thought maybe we were just crazy, or telling stories to entertain them. So my friends suggested we do an experiment to try to contact Mrs. Micks with a Ouija board.

(What do you think, would you have done this?)

Well, try as we might to communicate, or instigate some response, Mrs. Micks was silent. My friends were starting to make fun of my stories about her, teasing that I hadn't been truthful.

At that, I did become mad. I yelled an obscenity at Mrs. Micks, which made my buddies laugh, of course—until suddenly the whole house started shaking and banging! My friends were terrified and we all ran out of that house, laughing only after we were safely outside and everything seemed still again.

Our own relatives didn't believe the stories, because really, who would? Until one Thanksgiving, when a doubting but helpful cousin joined us in the kitchen to help with the after-dinner dishes. She taunted us about her disbelief of our dinner table tales. Just as she was speaking, a covered dish resting on the counter next to her flew off the counter and crashed into the wall!

She would repeat this story and say she would never doubt us again.

As we all grew older, I no longer lived in the house, but came over often to visit and care for my mother and after her death, for her husband. During their lives, they continued to have experiences with Mrs. Micks.

She seemed harmless enough. Once they were looking for their stomach upset medication. They kept their pills on a shelf in the kitchen cabinet, but could not find the package. They then heard a banging on the outside of the house. It sounded as if someone were bouncing a ball against the house. As they sat and listened, the kitchen cabinet door opened and the medicine fell out of the cabinet, as the banging stopped. It seemed Mrs. Micks was helping!

At Christmas time my wife and I visited. My stepfather had dozed in a chair in front of the television. Suddenly he woke up and stared. He went gray, all the blood drained from his face. "Don't you see her?" He said a little old lady was holding a gift out toward him. We saw nothing. He said that he had never believed it really, but now, he had actually seen her.

My mother finally died in the house. After her death I continued to stop by to check on my stepfather. Unfortunately on one such visit, I found the man dead on the bathroom floor.

Moving On

So we had to clean and prepare the house for sale. We cleaned and cleaned and cleaned, and left the house spotless. Before leaving the house, we took one last look around. Everything was immaculate. We left a few glasses neatly on the counter to dry. When we returned, a human tooth had been left on the counter! My wife was afraid to return to the house alone after that.

Just before we closed on a sale of the house, I met my brother at the house to check on it. The furnace was cranked up to 93 degrees. It was sweltering. We tried to turn it off. It would not turn off. The emergency shutoff just did not work. We had a repairman to the house. He was able to shut it down and restore it to normal, and it checked out; nothing was wrong with the furnace.

I had a dream that I figured out why Mrs. Micks was haunting. I just felt in my bones that she was haunting the house because she'd stashed money under the floor in the attic.

I never ripped up the floor to find out.

Before transferring the house, we had a Reiki therapist to the house to "clean" it out. He said the house was now clear of any lingering spirits. I never believed in that stuff. But the house seemed to be quiet afterwards, as far as I know. Or maybe, Mrs. Micks now has the company of my parents, who had also died in the house.

The people who bought the house flipped it immediately.

MURDER HOUSE:

HOME SWEET HOME

I was new to bamboo. Even with severed roots, bamboo had figured out how to keep growing. Even after I ripped out long sections of it from the hard dry ground, the damn bamboo kept pushing up shoots day after day. Had we seen it the day our agent showed us the place we would have reconsidered. Maybe. In fact, neither I nor my mother even noticed the backyard when we toured the house as our agent hurried us along, because there was another agent waiting with her client in a car parked out front. The nature of the market at the time required both buyers and sellers to act fast. Plus, we'd already sold our house and were two weeks away from becoming desperate and settling for something that didn't suit us.

This house was such a good deal, too, that all I saw in the yard were bushes, a fence and two sheds and a detached garage screaming, "storage, storage, storage!" Now, two months into the place, I cannot believe I never noticed the bamboo running wild, swallowing up the other bushes, spreading into the yard, under the sidewalk, pushing up cement. Cement!

Once I decided to address the situation, I did what I always do when faced with committing plant murder in the name of beautifying a yard. I shut down. Went numb. I'd been a landscaper, gardener, and typical human for much of my life and I knew that if it never occurs to you that the plant or tree is a living thing it's quite easy, and sometimes even satisfying, to rip it out of the soil or to saw through its trunk. Never mind the sap that oozes out like tears. Or the aroma of the thing's lifeblood, its essence, mostly a glorious smell. *Don't notice. Don't let it register. Just do your job. Not my fault I have to do my job. I need to pay my bills. Eat. Everyone else does it.*

After days and days of lopping off the long stalks, piercing their tangled roots with my shale bar and pick ax, prying and twisting, ripping with all my might only for it to break off and leave me with six inches of root in my hand, my back and shoulders hurt. My ego too. I would *not* be defeated by this aggressor onto my land, *my* yard. I had to kill it. It was pissing me off. *Who in hell planted it in the first place?*

And then, fearing for its life, a beetle, a tiny beautiful shiny black beetle, scurried across the violated soil. I leaned my shovel against the fence and knelt down on one knee to see him better. He was adorable and kind of like a cartoon, the way specks of dirt flew from his stick feet on stick legs as he sprinted up a miniature mountain. This always happened. Eventually something, like a little innocent beetle, would trigger my heart into feeling the violence in my own hands. It was awful. I hated it. No amount of justifying changed the fact that I was murdering the bamboo who just wanted to live, to be true to its nature, just like the rest of us.

So I stopped, defeated, at least for the day, and feeling bad about myself. There were plenty of other things to do anyway. Like hooking up the new washer and dryer, which first required my prying off the baseboard so they fit in the allotted washer-dryer space; because when I had measured, I measured from wall to wall, waist level, not on the floor. Old houses don't like new appliances.

And apparently, old plumbing doesn't like new appliances either. When I turned on the water, both the cold and the hot spigots leaked, dripping water down the back of the washer onto the floor. It was probably something I could have fixed with some plumber's tape, but since we had already scheduled a plumber to come fix a connection under the kitchen sink, I simply turned off the water to the washer and added the task to the plumber's list. Easy.

Despite these minor fixes throughout the 1939 craftsman house, and even with the bamboo ordeal, my mother and I really did love our new old house. She thought it would be the perfect last house for her and I thought it would be the perfect first house for me. It had character, history.

Yet, as with every move into a new living space, we had to ease into the feeling of it. It took time to adjust to the smells and sounds. The way the light shone into the different rooms. In the same way the walls and floors creaked in our last house, these walls and floors also creaked every so often. But unlike the creaking house we had just left to move here, this house wasn't a mere 50 yards away from a busy train track.

This house creaked, sometimes so loudly that I would be startled out of my meditation, or startled into alertness at night when I was trying to fall asleep. My mother noticed it too. We concluded that besides the normal heating and cooling throughout the day, the house was just easing into our being there. Our heavy walking up and down the steps, carrying weighty boxes, placing our furniture where none may have been before, hammering nails, (prying off molding). It was as if the house was getting used to us too.

It also took time to get used to the new views out of different windows and the habits of the community. The neighbor's wind chimes, church bells. The guy who cleaned the bank across the street late at night and always let the heavy lid of the dumpster slam down hard. The woman, decked out in bright neon green, who rode her bike every morning, her little trotting white dog in tow, through the intersection with hardly a look for cross traffic, always between 8:30 and 8:45. And then, of course, there were all the walkers. With dogs. Without. Our corner lot seemed to be the place where people crossed away from the house. Sometimes in the crosswalk, sometimes diagonally, as if they were in a hurry to their destination and needed to shave off some time.

Meeting the neighbors was also part of this easing into the place, this new scene that we would make home. Our first meeting happened over the short fence between yards. Both she and her husband were friendly, but like most strangers here upon first meeting, there was a noticeable barrier. A holding back. Waiting to see who the other was, and wasn't. The neighbors across the alley were friendly. Super chatty, as if they were a little nervous. I thought maybe high. He had a certain look to him. Plus he had started telling me how he used to jam with another guitar player in our garage and then his thoughts got derailed. It didn't matter. They were nice.

Only the neighbor across the street in the front was a little standoffish. I went right up and introduced myself when she came at a clip through her front yard chasing her grandson. She rounded him up and quickly retreated without saying much more than hello and welcome. I figured she had her hands full with her grandchildren or maybe there was something on the stove she needed to check on.

Mostly though, we found the people in our new community to be very friendly. Even guys on the job. The electrician. The couch delivery guys. And especially, the plumber. He finally arrived just when we both had a huge pile of dirty laundry and really didn't want to go to the laundromat yet again. He quickly sealed up the pipe under the kitchen sink and then started right in on replacing the faucets behind the washer. He was talkative. With little prompting from me, he went on about his path to becoming a plumber, and his frustration with the young people who don't want to put in the hours to learn the trade. He told us how he used to live in this neighborhood, just a few blocks away.

He paused for some air and then said he used to know the guy who lived here.

Our ears perked up. Of course we wanted to know everything there was to know about our new house and its history. He told us that the past owner used to own a pizza place across town, near his plumbing business, so he went there a lot for lunch. "Clint was a nice guy. Everyone liked him. Too bad."

So we asked, "Too bad? What happened?"

He kind of hesitated, then nonchalantly said, "Oh, he was murdered. By his son."

We gasped in unison. Unsure of what was insensitive or inappropriate, we didn't ask anything more and waited to see what he might offer. Somehow the conversation took a sharp right turn and he was telling us about how great Halloween is here, it's a big deal in this neighborhood, buy lots of candy. He gave his wrench one last turn and said, "Okay, that should do it," and turned on the water to make sure the connection was tight. He collected his tools and went outside to his truck to write up the bill. My mother followed him while I ran upstairs and got on the internet to find out if the history was really true.

Sure enough. It took mere seconds and the blood left my face. The newspaper article told the story. Eight bullets. One in the head. His son, suffering from mental illness, went off his medication. In *this* house. *This* house. I hurried down the stairs with my computer and met my mother in the kitchen. I didn't have to say a word. She could see it in my face, white as a ghost.

It took a day or two to digest this real story about a real father and son. We did some cathartic inappropriate laughing. We both sort of expected to have bad dreams or feel heavy energy, but we never did. From the beginning we felt fine in this house.

We also didn't notice the creaking anymore. Maybe because this wasn't about evil, but illness, which is just bad luck. Clint was a nice guy, no one to fear.

His son? Maybe it was like my bamboo struggle. Some alien thoughts had invaded his head and he acted violently in an effort at self-preservation. Maybe he had tried and tried to get rid of those invasive hungers but they kept coming back. Maybe he thought the roots of his infection lay deep in this family tree. He had confessed to his offense on the spot, and been institutionalized for treatment.

My mother and I smudged with sage and talked to Clint's spirit. We promised him we would love and take care of his house. Give it a new life. We would have friends over and laugh and prepare good food. I would keep tidy the garage and shop, and play music there with the neighbor and other musician friends I meet. We told him that we hoped his son got help for his illness and healed the violence in his hands.

Silently, to myself, I promised him I would do my best to be more tolerant and forgiving of my mother for the things that come between us. That I would do my best to heal my own familial wounds and to help her heal hers. We can fix the garden, together.

ANGELINE

My mother was a much loved wife and mother of five boys. She was very loving too, even though she had longed for a daughter as well, and had a girl's name in mind for each one of us before we were born. At birth we were given masculine names but we often teased each other with our "girl's" names. She had always had time to suspend her work for playing ball or other games with us.

Tragically she died too young of cancer, before I was married. My father was so distraught over her death that he was unable to speak her name again. As a family, we did not discuss her with each other because of our shared grief. It was only much later that we were able to share fond happy memories of her with our wives and children.

Many years later when I was grown and had my own family, we were all tucked in for the night in our cozy house in the woods. My wife was sound asleep next to me but I was unable to fall asleep.

Suddenly I saw an orb of light enter our room through the closed door. It hovered at the foot of my bed. It shone a green gold light, sparkling with stars; not as big as a person, no, just three feet high.

She was my mother. I don't know now if we spoke words to each other, or conversed within my mind or heart somehow. I don't know why she was so small; bodily, we were all taller than most. But I knew she was my mother. She asked about my children. I told her about my son and daughter asleep in their beds. She had come to visit and see our family. Seeing my family made her very happy.

All of a sudden there was an ice cold whoosh of air through the wall behind my bed. I felt that a giant hole had opened in the wall behind me. Even my sleeping wife mumbled, "Cold..." and pulled the blanket closer around her. The cold blast sucked my mother's orb of light over us in a whoosh and it was gone.

Then all was as before, our warm and cozy room. I was able to drift peacefully into sleep after the visit from my dear children's grandma, Angeline.

Over the next days, I was deeply moved with wondering over this visit. I kept it to myself for three weeks before I had the nerve to tell one of my brothers about my experience.

DEVIL'S CORNER

I n the old country, some people still
believe in devils roaming the earth
with us, and with so many witnesses, it
is little wonder why.

First Generation

Now perhaps you have heard of the
Carpathian Mountains. They have been
settled by Slavic peoples over many centuries,

and the borders have been made and revised through history between countries like Slovakia, Ukraine, Poland, Hungary, Romania. The Carpathians continue the Alps on the east and are bounded by the Balkans on the south. And you have probably heard of spooky stories out of the Transylvanian Alps, which are the southern Carpathians.

My family originated there, and back in the old country, in the old days, when my grandpa and grandma were a young married couple, there was no business in the country, no way to earn income. The way they would make money was to grow crops or take animals to sell at the market. My grandparents would go out and trap animals and then travel with their catch to bargain over prices in an open air market on market day.

On the southern slope of the Carpathians is a city called Uzhgorod, where the market would happen, and one night after my grandparents were out trapping, they traveled in their horse cart overnight to Uzhgorod, to sell the skins and flesh of the animals they had captured.

Grandma was sleeping, as Grandpa drove the cart bumping down the road, down into a valley, dropping
toward the river. The mountain was on one side of the road, a steep fall on the other.

Suddenly the horses stopped. They started acting very weird, and Grandpa had never seen them act like that. He jumped down from the wagon, trying to control them and push them back on the road. They would not go forward, the horses just wanted to go down the hill to the ditch! They would not survive the fall.

Grandpa screamed at her for help, but no amount of his noise could wake up Grandma. He climbed the hill a little ways himself to the crossroad. When he reached the cross, he heard some awful thing, screeching a terrible unnatural sound right at him. The unholy sound swooped down at his head and passed right on down the side of the mountain into the distance, into the deep gully.

And then, suddenly, it was quiet. The horses relaxed, and he was able to get the horses under control, so they proceeded on their way. Grandma slept through it all.

Grandpa remained upset about her sleeping through it, to the day he died.

Second Generation

But in the next generation, when my own mother was a teen, one night she was taking a shower in her building at just about midnight. Some people were already asleep and others were still up and about, clearing away their dinners and the day.

Suddenly, she heard a terrible caterwauling just outside the window. It wasn't just tomcats fighting, it was so awfully loud; it sounded like a terrible inhuman battle of some kind, with screams and screeches. She saw nothing outside in the darkness. She leapt away from the window and into her bed and drew the covers over her wet head. The supernatural cat fight sounds continued but finally faded out, or she fell asleep.

The next morning she asked everyone she could find in her building complex if they had heard the noise, or if there were any cats out in the neighborhood last night. (The walls in her building were thin and you could always hear all the neighbors; and everyone had their windows on that side of the building, and slept with them open.) All denied having heard a thing, and denied any cats or other animals, or evidence of such, indoors or out.

Third Generation

Remembering this story still makes me feel frightened when I think of it, to this day!

When I was about nine or ten years old, we raised rabbits for food. One day, at about noon, we went to the meadow as we often did, to turn the hay. The meadow slopes down, and you go down one side of the hay rows and then back up the other, and then you're done. We would do this to dry the hay to keep for our rabbits.

The people called this meadow "Devil's Corner". I had never thought anything about the name, it was just the name.

We were halfway through, when suddenly we heard a load of stones rolling through the mountains. We looked up at the mountain in fear. Then we heard a terrible sound, not human, but like no animal ever heard. It started as a roar and turned into an unearthly wailing. The wailing sound flew over our heads and through the entire valley, then went up, up, up, high into the woods at the top of mountain.

I ran like crazy. When you see your momma running, the one who is always brave and still and sane, you follow! We just dropped our rakes and we ran, from this weird sound flying through the valley.

We went home and told my grandparents our experience. They told us we were not the first ones to hear that. There had been a story people told about devils locally. And at Devil's Corner, somebody had died there in a way that had something to do with the falling stones. (They spoke quietly about this so I could not hear the details.) We had never heard the story before. My mother never told me stories like this.

I think when something happens like this, you don't forget it. I never heard it before or since, but I can still hear the sound in my head to this day! I don't like to think about it.

THE LOST RING

Our house stands on original American Semiahmoo land. My thoughts irresistibly turn to the People when I'm leaning against one of the big trees in our backyard.

This tree was here even 170 years ago. The ground we walk on is filled with the bones of our ancestors. How many trees began their long lives as tender roots in a puddle of nutrient rich blood? Does the energy of lives lived transmute the growing things, and the wood and brick and stone used in our buildings?

Things here in our house go missing a lot. I don't know if original residents are messing with me, or if I am followed by my own relatives.

My great-grandmother had a precious ring, a cats' eye. I didn't know her, but my grandmother had the ring, and she wore it, and she really, really wanted me to have it. In fact she passed it on to me when she was alive, and made me know I was to take special care of it, to hang on to it, that it was special and had great meaning for her.

After my grandmother had passed on, I spent a lot of time researching her family tree. I took great care with the ring, wrapped it carefully and kept it in a special box in the place in my desk where I kept my valuables and identity papers. In my research, I wasn't able to determine the meaning of the ring, but the names and dates and connections of family were precious to me. I looked up addresses and wrote letters to anyone I could find connected to the names on the tree.

Finally I discovered a 90 year old relative. So I sent her a card and a letter.

Two weeks later, her daughter called me. My letter was on her mother's bedside table, next to her when she died.

I wanted to help heal her grieving, so I offered her, with my sympathy for her loss, my great-grandmother's ring. This woman had children and grandchildren, and I have no heirs, so I thought I would try to keep the ring in the family line. She was thrilled to accept my offer of this token and seal of our family connection.

Well. The very next day I went for the ring, to wrap it and mail it. Wouldn't you know. It was gone! I looked everywhere. It cannot have been anywhere but in its special place; I would look at it sometimes but never remove it. I searched everywhere, tore apart the house, sifted trash and the vacuum cleaner contents. It was nowhere to be found. I had to explain the loss to the bereaved woman.

I didn't find the ring again, until one day when I read online an obituary notice for the relative to whom I had offered to give the ring. I went to add this detail to my family tree research kept in the place the ring had been— and there it was! As I had left it long before my frantic search, as if the ring had always been there and never left its place.

My grandmother really wanted to keep that ring with me! Or did other resident spirits borrow it, and return it to me when I needed to touch family again?

MY UNCLE'S VISIT

My mother had a brother just a year or two older. Her relationship with Joseph was strained, she never knew the reason. Perhaps he had felt angry when she was born, jealous about the new baby, and never recovered. Joseph was much loved and handsome and a wonderful person; but he and my mother were estranged, and we had not seen him in years.

Until he died.

My uncle had died in an accident in which he sacrificed his own safety at sea to save another soul.

My parents later told me this story about the next time they saw him.

You would believe them if you knew my parents. My father is a scientist and skeptic. There is nothing of which he is afraid, he has a healthy scientific curiosity regarding all mysterious events, and can figure out the real scientific reason why something appeared to happen. He can dismiss an unexplained happening and ruin all a kid's shivers, just like that.

My mother is not a fantasist. She does not read or view romances, fantasies, science fiction, horror. She prefers a face-to-face chat with a real person. She is an intelligent, hardworking, practical person, who can craft anything and is a perfectionist in her results.

My brother and I sleep upstairs. My parents' bedroom is on the first floor at the end of the hall. The other doors on this hallway are the cellar door and the back door out of the house. From their room, they had a view of the living room leading to the stairs which went up to our room.

Not too long after my uncle's death, in the middle of the night, when we were all in bed asleep and my parents were as well, my mother saw her brother.

He walked up the stairs from the cellar, turned right, and walked to her bedroom. He hesitated at her door for a long moment, looking in. He filled the doorway.

Then he turned away and walked to the stairs, going up and up and up the stairs.

She did not get out of bed. She knew her brother was not really upstairs in our house. She said, "George, I just saw my brother."

My father said, "I saw him, too."

THE BOY

WHO WANTED

POWER

When my mother was a teen, she experienced peculiar things in her village in the old country. But she also considered herself a "modern woman" who did not believe "all that superstitious gibberish". So when she recounts her experiences to me, the tales shake her to her core.

When she was still a small girl, they did not have power yet in their town. They lived, it seemed, at the end of the world. So power did not reach them there.

A nearby town had finally received electricity connection, but well before our village.

Now in those days there used to be "town criers," or "wailers", people who moaned and wailed with grief at funerals, in honor of the dead. Our little village was so small and busy with making our sustenance that we did not have people who served this function of loud and public grieving.

But there was one little boy, nine years old, who was very upset and envious that the next village had power, and we did not. And so he began wailing. We were not used to this sound and everyone was very alarmed when we heard this. He wailed and wailed for two whole weeks!

He started making "graves" for everyone in the town, and he made crosses which he stuck in the ground. The red thread from people's embroidery work in progress began to go missing; he kept stealing the red yarn to wrap onto and hang from crosses. Everyone in the village was so disturbed by him!

There was a man in town, considered a seer; people would go to him for advice, and he was often right. People said, well, he reads the Bible a lot, so he gets messages from God. Had he been a woman, I have no doubt they might have feared her as a witch, but he was considered a holy man.

So some of the villagers went to the seer and asked him what the child's behavior could mean.

The wise man said something bad is going to happen. There is going to be a fight; or death would come and take the young people, or something terrible like that. People blessed themselves, went out and muttered to each other about it, and the warning got around. They went home and shut themselves in for the night.

The next day was the boy's tenth birthday. Now this was a small village, and all hands were needed. The children would commonly tend the animals, take the livestock out into the fields to graze. The boy's grandmother asked him to take her goat out to the field. He didn't want to, because it was his birthday. So she offered him money to do his chore, and as a birthday gift. And so he went out with the goat, and brought a friend with him.

Well we do not know what talk passed between the boys, but somehow they ended up at the next town, the electrified town. And there was that transformer. And that boy decided he would climb up and try to unplug the town. He climbed the transformer, and he was fried.

The townspeople saw him. Everyone came to see. The people saw him hanging from the transformer, covered in charred blood. My grandmother saw it.

My grandmother, who was a child then remember, kept having dreams about that sight. She couldn't deal with it. She went to her grandmother and told her about her dreams. Her grandmother said some things to her, I don't what, which soothed her and then she was suddenly fine, and went on to live her life in peace.

Years later, when she had turned 12 years old, an age when children worked even harder, she was out working in a field. It was noon and she was hot. She stopped for a break and she fell asleep.

In the hot noon, she dreamed about the boy again, the first time after so long, and she was startled and glad to wake up. But somehow the sleep took her over again and she continued to drowse. The dream resumed. But now the boy had come down from the transformer and started to run after her. He chased her and got close enough to beat at her legs with a hazelnut stick.

If you do not know hazelwood, it is very hard and strong. In some cultures the hazel is thought to be sacred or magical, or to bring wealth or wisdom.

But this beating hurt, and my grandmother, the girl, woke up with marks and bruises all over her legs, as if she had been beaten with a stick.

UNCLE ALDO

My mother immigrated to New York from Italy as a beautiful young woman with her brother Aldo. They were both well educated for the time and place of their circumstances, with a taste for art and culture, philosophy and politics, salon conversation as it were.

While my mother married an American businessman and raised a family, Uncle Aldo pursued his independent and creative life. He was an opinionated writer, critic and artist. He entertained society and underground artists and personalities. But he maintained his family relationships and we all loved the visits from this striking, refreshingly unique and outspoken uncle. We loved to quote his sharp insights to spark a conversation even when he wasn't with us.

Sometimes he went dark for a while. A family curse and the strain of his intense lifestyle would result in his withdrawal from company, and we suspected episodes of some kind of health challenge.

But he always got better and returned to recapture the spotlight in any gathering.

Until the day he didn't. Suddenly he was gone. The family dealt with his estate. He had left his books and papers and artworks to me. Perhaps he saw me as a sympathetic spirit, some potential in me, in my photography, my work in publishing, my interests in theatre and dance. I felt honored.

Many years passed as I cared for my own family and for my mother. One night, I experienced what I must assume was a dream. But it "looked" and felt like no dream I had ever had in my lifetime.

I woke in the middle of the night in what had been a dark room. There in the middle of the room was my own Uncle Aldo. However, he was wearing the most beautiful jacket I had ever seen. More than beautiful. It was indeed indescribable. He was bright and shining, emitting light which almost hurt my eyes. I cannot tell you the many varied colors of his jacket, because they were unique colors I had never before seen in my human lifetime on earth. They were such deep, rich, intense colors you could fall into and almost feel, but at the same time there was so much brightness. He was like, this is strange but I felt like he was a star, fallen into my bedroom and standing there, a star emitting light and color and energy, and the color was such that I had never seen anything like it.

And he spoke to me. He asked me sternly about his books and papers and things. He asked me how I was doing with organizing them. He asked if they were within my attention yet.

I sat up awake with a chill, and the room went dark.

I tell friends about this dream as the most unearthly experience of my life, and most everyone shudders and claims this was no dream.

This was a visit.

I leave these facts behind me, and if you can explain them, do so; or if you choose to doubt them, do so. Neither your belief nor your incredulity can alter them...

--Arthur Conan Doyle,
     The Terror of Blue John Gap

About Salt 'n' Pepper Books

Salt and Pepper are cousins. They played together growing up and named themselves Salt 'n' Pepper, because they came to the table together and were better together. Together they added spice to the cousins' invented games, sport and play. All the cousins loved music and physical feats and jokes and campfire tales. There were many storytellers through many generations in their family, and they listened and soaked up the stories.

Now that Salt and Pepper are grown, they love to investigate and share the weird and wild truths that captivated them as kids.

Made in United States
Troutdale, OR
08/19/2023

12214355R00083